CONTENTS

THE ROMAN EMPIRE

Nearly 3,000 years ago, the **population** of the Italian city of Rome started to grow. Rome became the most powerful city in Italy. The people from Rome (the Romans) began to control the whole country.

Many Roman buildings, such as the Colosseum, still stand in Italy today. In Roman times, people visited the Colosseum to watch **gladiator** fights.

FACT CAT

ROMAN BRITAIN

Izzi Howell

WAYLAND
www.waylandbooks.co.uk

FACT CAT

Get your paws on this fantastic new mega-series from Wayland!

Join our Fact Cat on a journey of fun learning about every subject under the sun!

First published in Great Britain in 2015 by Wayland
Copyright © Wayland 2015

ISBN: 978 0 7502 9582 6
Dewey Number: 936.1'04-dc23

10 9 8 7 6 5 4 3 2 1

MIX
Paper from responsible sources
FSC® C104740

Wayland
An imprint of Hachette Children's Group
Part of Hodder & Stoughton
Carmelite House
50 Victoria Embankment
London EC4Y 0DZ

An Hachette UK Company
www.hachette.co.uk
www.hachettechildrens.co.uk

A catalogue for this title is available from
the British Library
Printed and bound in China

Produced for Wayland by
White-Thomson Publishing Ltd
www.wtpub.co.uk

Editor: Izzi Howell
Design: Rocket Design (East Anglia) Ltd
Fact Cat illustrations: Shutterstock/Julien Troneur
Other illustrations: Stefan Chabluk
Consultant: Kate Ruttle

Picture and illustration credits:
Corbis: Heritage Images 7 and 10, Stefano Bianchetti 14, The Print Collector 20; iStock: Anthony Brown 11b, BrettCharlton 12; Shutterstock: yahiyat (cover), Laurence Gough (title page), KKulikov 4, Regien Paassen 6, verityjohnson 8, stocksolutions 9, Laurence Gough 13, Iuri 15, Hein Nouwens 16, mountainpix 17t, cpaulfell 18, Andrei Nekrassov 19, ChameleonsEye 21; Stefan Chabluk: 5; Wikimedia: Walters Art Museum (acquired in 1930) 11t and 17b.

Every effort has been made to clear copyright.
Should there be any inadvertent omission,
please apply to the publisher for rectification.

The author, Izzi Howell, is a writer and editor specialising in children's educational publishing.

The consultant, Kate Ruttle, is a literacy expert and SENCO, and teaches in Suffolk.

FACT CAT FACT

There is a question for you to answer on each spread in this book. You can check your answers on page 24.

Over the next 500 years, the Romans took control of many countries in Europe, the Middle East and North Africa. These countries followed Roman **laws** and spoke Latin, the Roman language. Even though their **empire** was large, the Romans always wanted more land to control.

BRITAIN
London ○

Atlantic Ocean

Caspian Sea

Black Sea

ITALY
□ Rome

Mediterranean Sea

☐ Roman Empire in 117CE

This map shows the Roman Empire in 117CE, when the empire was at its largest.

FACT CAT FACT

The Romans controlled an area that is divided into 54 countries today, from Portugal in the west to Iraq in the east. What was the Roman name for Portugal?

THE ROMANS ARRIVE IN BRITAIN

The Romans first tried to **invade** Britain in 55BCE. The **Celts**, who controlled Britain at that time, beat the Romans in battle. Nearly 100 years later, **Emperor** Claudius invaded Britain again. This time, the Romans **defeated** the Celts and began to take control of southern Britain.

We think that Roman soldiers wore armour like this. Emperor Claudius sent over 40,000 Roman soldiers to invade Britain in 43CE.

FACT CAT FACT

Emperor Claudius ordered that an elephant should be part of the army that invaded Britain. The Romans often used elephants in battles to scare their enemies.

After the Roman **invasion**, Britain became part of the Roman Empire. Romans from all over the empire came to Britain to live alongside the Celts. Some Celts were unhappy about being ruled by Romans. They tried to fight back but each time the Romans defeated them.

This drawing shows the Celts attacking the town of Londinium, known today as London. What was the name of the Celtic queen who led a **rebellion** against the Romans?

HADRIAN'S WALL

Northern Britain and Scotland were not part of the Roman Empire. Scottish **tribes** would sometimes attack Roman Britain. In 122CE, Emperor Hadrian decided to build a high wall across the north of England to control who could enter the country.

Hadrian's Wall was between five and six metres tall. It ran for nearly 120km from the east coast to the west coast of England.

Soldiers lived in forts along Hadrian's Wall. They **patrolled** up and down the wall to make sure nobody climbed over.

Parts of Hadrian's Wall can still be seen today. These are the remains of a milecastle, a type of small fort.

AROUND TOWN

The Romans built towns all over Britain, connected by straight roads. They built their new towns in the same style and layout as the towns in the rest of their empire. In the town centre, there was always a large open market called a **forum**. Town meetings took place in a **basilica**, next to the forum.

This is a drawing of the Roman town of Londinium. In Roman times, there was a wooden bridge across the River Thames.

forum

Londinium was one of the largest towns in Roman Britain. However, its population of 60,000 people is much smaller than the population of London today, which is 8.4 million people!

The Romans built shops, **temples** and **public baths** in their towns. Rich Romans went to the public baths several times a week to clean themselves and meet their friends. Public baths had hot, warm and cold baths and outdoor gyms.

To keep clean, the Romans would cover themselves in olive oil at the public baths and then get a **slave** to scrape off the oil and dirt using this tool, called a strigil.

The Roman baths in Bath are still standing today. What was the Roman name for the city of Bath?

HOUSES AND VILLAS

The Romans brought new ideas about house building to Britain. Celtic houses were made from wood, mud and straw. Roman houses were made from brick and stone.

These are the remains of a Roman house's central heating system. The floor was built on top of tall stones with an empty space below. Hot air was pumped into the empty space under the floor to keep the house warm.